BASIC SKILLS

HAL LEONARD STUDENT P

Ear Withou...

Volume 1

A Comprehensive Ear-Training Program for Musicians

CW00385887

TABLE OF CONTENTS

ISBN-13: 978-0-634-08799-8

HAL LEONARD®
CORPORATION

7777 W. BLUEMOUND RD. P.O. BOX 13819 MILWAUKEE, WI 53213

Visit Hal Leonard Online at
www.halleonard.com

A Note to Students

You will find this series easy to use. To use the books effectively, you will need a pitch pipe or your instrument and a CD player.

Each chapter is divided into smaller sections. This allows you to focus on one section for a short period of time. Working in small sections is more valuable than trying to cover large amounts of material. Learning this way lays a good foundation as you continue to build your skills.

All exercises and dictations may be used repeatedly for additional practice or review. For written exercises, you may either erase your answers or use a separate sheet of paper.

YOUR CD:
- You may access tracks on your CD by moving from smaller numbers up or from larger numbers down. Simply press the track buttons to find the desired track number.
- ▶▶| This button will move forward through the CD.
- |◀◀ This button will move backward through the CD. Larger numbers may easily be reached by moving backward from Track 1 while the CD is playing.
- The dictations and exercises are played once. Repeat tracks as many times as necessary to complete each exercise.

YOUR WORKBOOK:

All of the chapters are set up in the same way. Labeled headings appear on the left-hand side of the page. These headings introduce a series of tasks designed to familiarize you with various melodic concepts and patterns.

LISTENING

Under this heading, your CD will provide exercises that will train your ear, as shown below.

Exercise A   H – The second pitch or sound is higher than the first.

Exercise B   L – The second pitch or sound is lower than the first.

IDENTIFYING

This next heading provides you with exercises on the CD to listen to and new concepts to practice. You will usually need to fill in the blanks, providing the answers based on what you hear.

DICTATION

This heading contains a series of exercises in which you will write down the melodic patterns that you hear.

On the CD, you will hear each dictation once. Repeat the tracks as often as necessary to complete each exercise. Simply listen the first time, then complete the dictations as instructed.

1.

2.

3.

NEW ELEMENT

New musical concepts will be introduced under this heading.

Do is written on the second line from the bottom of the staff.

Re is written in the second space.

MATCHING

Under this heading, you will see a series of boxes containing melodic patterns. You will match the pattern you hear on the CD by indicating the corresponding letter in the space provided.

A    B

C 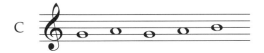   D

E    F

1. _____   2. _____   3. _____

4. _____   5. _____   6. _____

SIGHT-SINGING

This heading provides an opportunity for you to sing, at first sight, a series of pitches notated on the staff. To begin each exercise, you will need to play the first pitch on your instrument or pitch-pipe.

It is important to sing the exercises in a range where they sit most comfortably in your voice.

1. 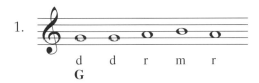   2.

Remember, with the exercises and dictations, accuracy is what counts. Speed will come later.

You and your teacher may want to chart your progress. Try keeping a log showing the number of times you had to listen to the exercises before completing them and how accurately you were able to do sight-singing exercises the first time through.

We recommend that you use the companion series:

Rhythm Without the Blues

Rhythm Without the Blues is a comprehensive rhythm-training program. Using these two series together will help you to master the dictations and exercises in Volumes 2, 3, 4, and 5 with success.

A Note to Teachers

Ear Without Fear is an innovative program aimed at building a foundation for reading music and developing the skills to perform it accurately.

Ear training demands heightened listening skills that involve hearing and understanding pitch differentiation. Ear training is distinct from rhythm, which is mathematical in structure and employs different neurological pathways. Because both elements are invariably placed together in music training, the result is often frustration and a sense of failure. In this series, these elements are ultimately combined. However, rhythm is not used in Volume 1. Volumes 2, 3, 4, and 5 provide exercises that integrate melodic and rhythmic components.

Educators have long known that step-by-step learning is essential. A sense of accomplishment and confidence at each level is the motivating force behind the desire to continue. It is assumed at the beginning of Volume 1 that the student may have no prior experience with ear training; therefore, the first few chapters cover the basics. Some students, particularly those who have studied an instrument, may already have developed an understanding of these concepts. Because of this, a minimum amount of time may be spent on these basics. The balance of the book offers demonstrations, listening exercises, sight-singing, and melodic dictations which will help even experienced students to reinforce and hone melodic skills.

We have carefully chosen and organized the materials in this book to make the learning process as accessible to students as possible. The Workbook and the CDs are integrated to provide several learning approaches: AURAL, VISUAL, and PRACTICAL. Together, they present a comprehensive, step-by-step learning program for which the student can assume primary responsibility.

The following concepts will be covered in Volume 1:

- high and low pitch differentiation

- ascending and descending notes and phrases

- introduction of the treble staff

- introduction of tonic sol-fa

- demonstrations, exercises, and dictations covering these areas

These materials make use of the Tonic Sol-fa music reading system developed by British educator and publisher John Curwen (1816–1880). Sol-fa facilitates pitch recognition and differentiation.

- It provides a prepared curriculum.

- Students can work independently with well-formatted, easily-understood exercises.

- Chapters are easily divided for appropriately-sized weekly assignments.

- Exercises and dictations are readily available for weekly testing and instruction.

- Lesson time is maximized for instrumental instruction, while ensuring that the student is honing musicianship skills.

Students often find the development of essential rhythm and ear training skills less exciting than learning an instrument, so a reward system may be helpful. Consider implementing one, using some of these suggestions:

- Encourage student to keep a log outlining the number of sections and exercises completed over the week. They may also want to keep track of how long it takes to complete each exercise. Students' confidence will grow as they begin to see an increase in proficiency and speed.

- Award incentive points for successful completion of sections and increased proficiency. Give prizes and awards based on accumulated points.

It is recommended that students also use the companion series:

Rhythm Without the Blues is a comprehensive rhythm-training program that works in tandem with *Ear Without Fear.* Using them together will greatly enhance the ability of the student to master successfully the dictations and exercises contained in each series.

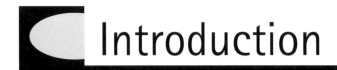

Introduction

Melody

Melody is like a train taking us through a mountain range. Sometimes we move up a long incline or down a steep hill. Sometimes the train moves straight through a meadow or wends its way around the mountain side. Listen to an excerpt of Mozart's overture to *The Marriage of Figaro*, on track 1.

 PLAY CD TRACK 1

It is a thrilling experience to ride the train through the mountains. We have just listened and discovered what an equally thrilling experience it is to let the melody take you on an exciting journey.

In this series, *Ear Without Fear*, we will begin to discover melody and its movement. We will also train our ear to listen and discern the subtle ways in which the composer has used melodic patterns to communicate through the music.

Moods like joy, sorrow, and excitement are conveyed through music. Melodic movement is one of the components of that communication process.

In training our ear to hear how the melody moves, we break down the process into small steps. We first need to know whether the melody line is moving up or down. Then we need to train our ear to know by how much it is moving up or down. Finally, we hone our skills by listening to and writing out the melodic patterns.

By training our ear in this way, we begin to develop the ability to sight-sing a melodic line. This musicianship skill is important, no matter what your chosen instrument might be.

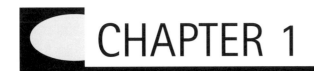

CHAPTER 1

High and low sounds

LISTENING

Whether the notes are moving higher or lower than the preceding ones determines the pathway, or movement, of a tune or melody. Listen to the following familiar tune, "Frère Jacques."

PLAY CD TRACK 2

While you may not be able to identify when the notes are going up and when they are going down, you are probably aware that the notes are moving around.

In order to trace the direction of a melody, we will need to develop a good sense of high and low sounds. Listen to the following two selections on track 3.

PLAY CD TRACK 3

Which one sounds high and which one sounds low? You probably said that in the first selection, the flute sounds high and light, while in the second selection, the French horn has a darker and heavier sound.

Listen to the next two examples (played one after the other) and determine which one you think is higher and which one is lower.

PLAY CD TRACK 4

In this case, the baritone singer was definitely lower in pitch. The second singer, a soprano, had higher and brighter sounds. Now listen to two notes played on the piano.

PLAY CD TRACK 5

If you said the second note was higher than the first, you are correct. You may want to listen to these examples again.

So far, we've used the terms "pitch" and "note," which basically mean the same thing and can be used interchangeably.

Listen and follow along with Exercises A–D. Each exercise will be played once, with the second note being pitched either higher (H) or lower (L) in contrast.

PLAY CD TRACK 6

Exercise A   H – The second pitch or sound is higher than the first.

Exercise B   L – The second pitch or sound is lower than the first.

Exercise C   L – The second pitch or sound is lower than the first.

Exercise D   H – The second pitch or sound is higher than the first.

IDENTIFYING

In the following exercises, if the second sound is higher in pitch than the first, indicate this with an "H." If the second sound is lower in pitch, indicate this with an "L." Play the track for each group of two pitches, one at a time. If you need to listen again, simply repeat the track. Answers are on page 31.

GROUP A

PLAY CD TRACK 7

1. _____   2. _____   3. _____

4. _____   5. _____

GROUP B

PLAY CD TRACK 8

6. _____   7. _____   8. _____

9. _____   10. _____

PLAY CD TRACK 9

11. _____   12. _____   13. _____

14. _____   15. _____

PLAY CD TRACK 10

16. _____   17. _____   18. _____

19. _____   20. _____

After checking your answers, if you have succeeded in 18 out of 20 of the exercises, proceed to the next chapter.

If there are still difficulties, review the chapter and redo the exercises, listening carefully. Doing these exercises several times is a good idea, because training your ear requires frequent repetition.

CHAPTER 2

Ascending and descending phrases

Now that we have developed our skills in determining high and low sounds, let's begin to identify which direction a series of notes is taking.

A melody, or series or pitches, can move in two directions: ASCENDING (up) and DESCENDING (down). Ascending pitches move higher from the starting pitch. Descending pitches move lower from the starting pitch. The following directional shorthand will be used frequently throughout this book:

DIRECTIONAL SHORTHAND

∧ This symbol indicates "ascending"

∨ This symbol indicates "descending"

LISTENING

In the following exercises, some melodies are ascending and some are descending. Listen carefully to help train your ear to hear the differences in direction.

PLAY CD TRACK 11

Exercise A   ∧   Ascending – The pitches are moving up.

Exercise B   ∧   Ascending – The pitches are moving up.

Exercise C   ∨   Descending – The pitches are moving down.

Exercise D   ∨   Descending – The pitches are moving down.

IDENTIFYING

In the following exercises, use the directional shorthand to indicate whether the melody is ascending or descending. Play the track for each group. If you need to listen again, simply repeat the track. Answers are on page 31.

GROUP A

PLAY CD TRACK 12

1. _____   2. _____

3. _____   4. _____

GROUP B

PLAY CD TRACK 13

5. _____   6. _____

7. _____   8. _____

GROUP C

PLAY CD TRACK 14

9. _____   10. _____

11. _____   12. _____

After checking your answers, if you have succeeded in 11 out of 12 of the exercises, proceed to the next chapter. If there are still difficulties, review the chapter and do the exercises again, listening carefully.

CHAPTER 3

Ascending and descending phrases within a melody

Melodies can be divided into segments. Some melodic segments ascend and some descend. When they are combined, they create variety within the melody.

The next step is to begin to develop a sense of how the melody is moving. When are the notes going up and when are they coming down? In the following excerpt from a piano piece by the Russian composer Vladimir Rebikov (1866-1920), we hear the melody ascend and then descend.

 PLAY CD TRACK 15

In the next excerpt by the Danish composer Niels Gade (1817-1890), we hear the melody descend and then ascend three times.

 PLAY CD TRACK 16

LISTENING

Listen to the following exercises, following the directional shorthand given for each one.

 PLAY CD TRACK 17

Exercise A   ∧ ∨   This melody ascends and then descends.

Exercise B   ∨ ∧   This melody descends and then ascends.

Exercise C   ∨ ∧   This melody descends and then ascends.

Exercise D   ∧ ∨   This melody ascends and then descends.

IDENTIFYING

In the following exercises, use the directional shorthand to indicate whether the melody is ascending (moving up) or descending (moving down). Play the track for each group, one at a time. Repeat the track if necessary. Answers are on page 31.

PLAY CD TRACK 18

1. _____ _____   2. _____ _____

3. _____ _____   4. _____ _____

PLAY CD TRACK 19

5. _____ _____   6. _____ _____

7. _____ _____   8. _____ _____

PLAY CD TRACK 20

9. _____ _____   10. _____ _____

11. _____ _____   12. _____ _____

After checking your answers, if you have succeeded in 11 out of the 12 exercises, proceed to the next chapter. If you still have difficulty, review the chapter and do the exercises again, listening carefully.

CHAPTER 4

Ascending and descending notes within a melody

The pitches in a melody also ascend or descend in relation to one another. This movement affects the overall direction of a melody.

So far, we have looked at the big picture: melodic segments that have a general movement up and down. Now we will take the melodic segments apart and see how individual notes relate to each other.

LISTENING

In the examples below, the note symbol indicates the first pitch you will hear. Whether the following note is higher or lower than the preceding pitch is indicated by the directional shorthand. Follow along with each exercise, listening for the directional changes.

PLAY CD TRACK 21

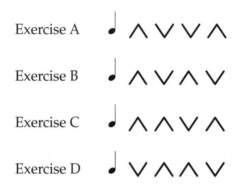

IDENTIFYING

In the following exercises, use the directional shorthand to indicate whether the pitches ascend or descend. Repeat the track if necessary. Answers are on page 31.

PLAY CD TRACKS 22–31

1. ♩ ___ ___ ___ ___

2. ♩ ___ ___ ___ ___

3. ♩ ___ ___ ___ ___

4. ♩ ___ ___ ___ ___

5. ♩ ___ ___ ___ ___

6. ♩ ___ ___ ___ ___

7. ♩ ___ ___ ___ ___

8. ♩ ___ ___ ___ ___

9. ♩ ___ ___ ___ ___

10. ♩ ___ ___ ___ ___

CHAPTER 5

Repeated notes within a melody

Sometimes the pitches in a melody do not ascend or descend—they stay the same. The following directional shorthand will be used to indicate when the pitches remain the same:

DIRECTIONAL SHORTHAND

— This symbol indicates "same"

LISTENING

Listen to the following exercises, paying close attention to when the melody ascends, descends, or stays the same.

PLAY CD TRACK 32

Exercise A   ♩ ∧ — ∨ ∧

Exercise B   ♩ ∨ ∨ — ∨

Exercise C   ♩ ∨ — ∧ ∧

Exercise D   ♩ ∧ ∨ ∨ —

IDENTIFYING

In the following exercises, use the directional shorthand to indicate whether the pitches ascend, descend, or remain the same. Repeat the track if necessary. Answers are on page 31.

PLAY CD TRACKS 33–42

1. ♩ ___ ___ ___ ___   2. ♩ ___ ___ ___ ___

3. ♩ ___ ___ ___ ___   4. ♩ ___ ___ ___ ___

5. ♩ ___ ___ ___ ___   6. ♩ ___ ___ ___ ___

7. ♩ ___ ___ ___ ___   8. ♩ ___ ___ ___ ___

9. ♩ ___ ___ ___ ___   10. ♩ ___ ___ ___ ___

CHAPTER 6

The staff

When melodies and pitches are written down, they are written on a STAFF. A staff is made up of five horizontal lines and four spaces.

At the beginning of the staff, you will find a TREBLE CLEF. A clef is used to determine the exact pitch of the notes written on the staff. The treble clef is the first clef we will use.

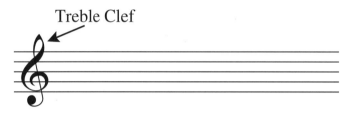

Pitches are indicated by writing notes on the staff. Notes are written on the lines and in the spaces as in the illustrations below. Notes that move from the bottom of the staff to the top of the staff (from left to right) are ascending. Notes that move from the top of the staff to the bottom of the staff are descending.

Music was first notated in the 9th century with small dots and squiggles called *neumes*. The neumes represented single notes or groups of notes. The staff was introduced in the 11th century and notation gradually developed from there. By the 17th and 18th centuries, notation was fairly standardized and looked more or less as it does today.

LISTENING

Listen to the following exercises, paying close attention to when the melody ascends, descends, or stays the same. Also notice the direction on the staff from one note to the next.

PLAY CD TRACK 43

DICTATION

Do the following exercises in two steps. First, using directional shorthand, indicate whether the pitches ascend, descend, or remain the same. Second, write in the notes, using the directional shorthand as a guide. Repeat the track if necessary. Answers are on page 31.

PLAY CD TRACKS 44–53

1.

2.

3.

4.

5.

6.

7.

8.

9.

10.

When you are finished, practice singing along with each track on the CD, listening and adjusting carefully to match each pitch with your voice.

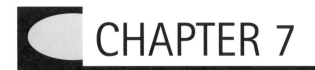

CHAPTER 7

Tonic sol-fa – d, r, m

In this chapter, we will begin to identify and recognize specific pitches. We will be using a system of music reading called TONIC SOL-FA to help us become familiar with the various pitches and their relationships to one another. The following shorthand will also be used.

TONIC SOL-FA SHORTHAND

d = do

r = re

m = mi

This system of music reading was developed by John Curwen, the 19th-century British music educator and publisher. He developed these syllables as a tool to help students learn to read music and to hear and recognize changes in pitch.

Listen to the "tonic sol-fa" in the following tune.

 PLAY CD TRACK 54

do re mi re do re mi mi re do re do do do

The familiar song "Do-Re-Mi" from Rodgers and Hammerstein's *The Sound of Music* also demonstrates the use of "tonic sol-fa."

We will begin by placing *do* on the second line of the staff.

NEW ELEMENT

Do is written on the second line from the bottom of the staff.

Re is written in the second space.

Mi is written on the third line.

LISTENING

Listen to each example, paying close attention to direction. Repeat the track and practice singing along, listening carefully to match each pitch with your voice.

 PLAY CD TRACK 55

Exercise A

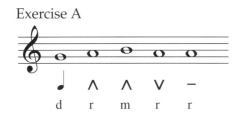

d r m r r

Exercise B

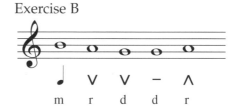

m r d d r

Exercise C

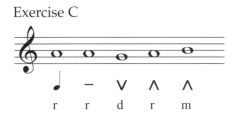

r r d r m

Exercise D

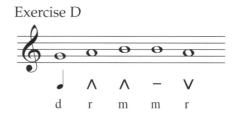

d r m m r

MATCHING

Listen to the tracks one at a time and find the matching melody box below. Write the letter of the matching box in the space provided. Repeat the track if necessary. Answers are on page 32.

 PLAY CD TRACKS 56–61

A

B

C

D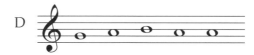

E

F

1. _____   2. _____   3. _____

4. _____   5. _____   6. _____

SIGHT-SINGING

For each of the following exercises, play the initial pitch on your instrument or pitchpipe. For example, the letter G is written under the first note of Exercise 1. This means to sound a G to establish the starting pitch. Sing each exercise twice, using tonic sol-fa. Check for accuracy on your instrument or pitchpipe. The first two exercises are demonstrated for you on the CD. To prepare, practice singing along with these tracks, listening carefully to match each pitch with your voice.

PLAY CD TRACK 62

It is important to sing the exercises in the range that is most comfortable for your voice.

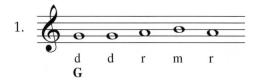

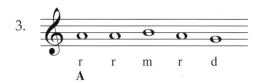

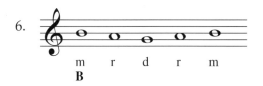

DICTATION

Play the tracks one at a time. Write the melodic pattern that you hear. The starting pitch is given. Fill in the directional shorthand first, followed by the sol-fa, then the notes. Repeat the track if necessary. Answers are on page 32.

PLAY CD TRACKS 63–68

1.

2.

3.

4.

5.

6.

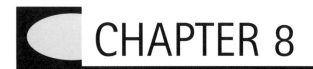

CHAPTER 8

Steps and skips

Our studies have shown how a melodic segment can be varied. The notes may ascend, descend, or remain on the same pitch. So far, the demonstrations and exercises have involved only pitches that move to the very next line or space. This movement is called a STEP. In this chapter, we will begin to train our ear to hear when the notes move by more than a single step. This movement is called a SKIP. The following directional shorthand will be used to indicate ascending and descending skips:

DIRECTIONAL SHORTHAND

∧^ This symbol indicates "skip up."

∨˅ This symbol indicates "skip down."

Notes that move stepwise will move to the very next line or space. Notes that skip will skip a line or space. The children's song "Hot Cross Buns" is made up of many steps and one skip up:

 PLAY CD TRACK 69: "HOT CROSS BUNS"

NEW ELEMENT

Do to *re* is a **Step** up.

Do to *mi* is a **Skip** up.

Mi to *re* is a **Step** down.

Mi to *do* is a **Skip** down.

LISTENING

Listen to each example, paying close attention to direction and distance (step or skip). Repeat the track and practice singing along, listening carefully to match each pitch with your voice.

 PLAY CD TRACK 70

Exercise A

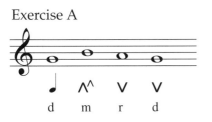

Exercise B

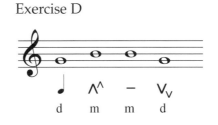

Exercise C

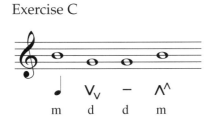

Exercise D

MATCHING

Listen to the tracks one at a time and find the matching tune below. Write the letter of the matching tune in the space provided. Repeat the track if necessary. Answers are on page 32.

 PLAY CD TRACKS 71–74

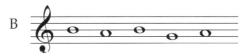

1. _____   2. _____

3. _____   4. _____

SIGHT-SINGING

For each of the following exercises, play the initial pitch on your instrument or pitchpipe. For example, the letter G is written under the first note of Exercise 1. This means to sound a G to establish the starting pitch. Sing each exercise twice, using tonic sol-fa. Check for accuracy on your instrument or pitchpipe. Exercise 1 is demonstrated for you on the CD.

PLAY CD TRACK 75

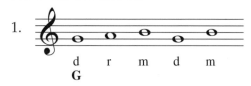

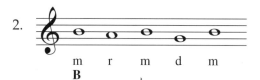

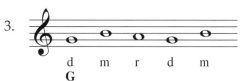

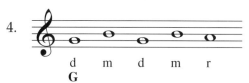

DICTATION

Play the tracks one at a time. Write the melodic pattern that you hear. The starting pitch is given. Fill in the directional shorthand first, followed by the sol-fa, then the notes. Repeat the track if necessary. Answers are on page 32.

PLAY CD TRACKS 76–81

REVIEW TEST

The following test consists of five parts, _____, _____, _____, _____, and _____. Total possible points for each section are listed to the left of each section heading. Answers are on page 32

Answers are on page 32

7 REVIEW QUESTIONS

Each answer is worth one point.

1. Another word for *note* is _____.

2. This symbol ∧ means the note or melodic line is _____.

3. A melodic line with pitches going down is said to be _____.

4. Sometimes pitches in a melody stay the same. What is the directional shorthand? _____

5. When a note moves to the very next line or space it is called a _____.

6. John Curwen developed a system of music reading called _____.

7. If there is more than one step between two notes it is called a _____.

Score: _____ out of 7

4 MATCHING

Listen to track 82 and find the matching tune for each example below. Each tune will be played twice. Write the letter of the matching tune in the space provided. Repeat the track if necessary. Each answer is worth one point.

PLAY CD TRACK 82

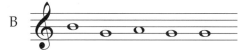

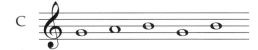

8. _____   9. _____   10. _____   11. _____

Score: _____ out of 4

IDENTIFYING

In the following exercises, use the directional shorthand to indicate whether the pitches ascend, descend, or remain the same. Repeat the track if necessary. Each answer is worth four points.

PLAY CD TRACKS 83–90

12. ♩ ____ ____ ____ ____

13. ♩ ____ ____ ____ ____

14. ♩ ____ ____ ____ ____

15. ♩ ____ ____ ____ ____

16. ♩ ____ ____ ____ ____

17. ♩ ____ ____ ____ ____

18. ♩ ____ ____ ____ ____

19. ♩ ____ ____ ____ ____

Score: _____ out of 32

6 SIGHT-SINGING

For each of the following exercises, play the initial pitch on your instrument or pitchpipe. Sing each exercise twice, using tonic sol-fa. Check for accuracy on your instrument or pitchpipe. Each answer is worth one point.

20.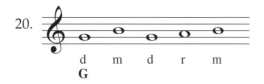
d m d r m
G

21.
m d r m d
B

22.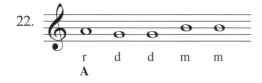
r d d m m
A

23.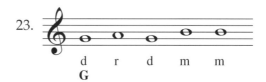
d r d m m
G

24.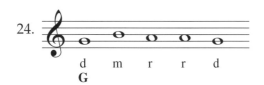
d m r r d
G

25.
m r d m r
B

Ask your teacher to check your accuracy and assign a score for this part of the review.

Score: _____ out of 6

DICTATION

Play the tracks one at a time. Since two exercises are on each track, pause the CD between exercises and rewind as necessary. Write the melodic pattern that you hear. Fill in the tonic sol-fa and then the notes. Repeat the track if necessary. Each question is worth five points. In order to receive a full point, you must correctly identify all three elements for each note: directional shorthand, tonic solfa, and note on the staff. If any one of these three elements is incorrect, subtract one point.

PLAY CD TRACK 91

26.   d

27.   m

PLAY CD TRACK 92

28.   d

29.   m

PLAY CD TRACK 93

30.   r

31.   d

PLAY CD TRACK 94

32.   m

33.   d

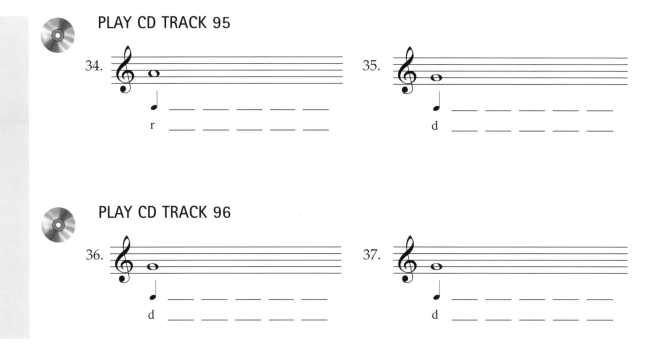

PLAY CD TRACK 95

34.

r

35.

d

PLAY CD TRACK 96

36.

d

37.

d

Score: _____ out of 60

TOTAL SCORE: _____ out of 109

If your score was 98 or better, Congratulations! You may proceed to

EAR WITHOUT FEAR VOLUME 2

If your score was 97 or less, you should review any elements
that gave you difficulty before continuing.

Learning to hear and identify is a fundamental skill.
Take the time to review and practice these exercises frequently as you continue to train your ear.

ANSWERS

CHAPTER 1

IDENTIFYING:

1. H	2. L	3. L	4. H	5. L
6. H	7. H	8. L	9. H	10. L
11. H	12. L	13. L	14. H	15. H
16. L	17. H	18. L	19. L	20. H

CHAPTER 2

IDENTIFYING:

1. ∧	2. ∧	3. ∨	4. ∧
5. ∨	6. ∨	7. ∧	8. ∧
9. ∨	10. ∧	11. ∨	12. ∨

CHAPTER 3

IDENTIFYING:

1. ∧∨	2. ∨∧	3. ∨∧	4. ∨∧
5. ∧∨	6. ∧∨	7. ∨∧	8. ∧∨
9. ∧∨	10. ∨∧	11. ∨∧	12. ∧∨

CHAPTER 4

IDENTIFYING:

1. ∧∨∨∧	2. ∧∨∧∨	3. ∧∧∨∨	4. ∨∧∧∨
5. ∨∧∨∧	6. ∧∨∨∧	7. ∧∨∧∧	8. ∨∧∧∨
9. ∧∨∨∨	10. ∧∧∨∨		

CHAPTER 5

IDENTIFYING:

1. ∧—∧∨	2. ∨∨—∧	3. —∨∨∧	4. ∧∨—∨
5. ∨∨∨—	6. ∧—∧∨	7. —∨—∨	8. ∨——∨
9. ∧——∨	10. ∨∧∧∧		

CHAPTER 6

DICTATION:

1.
     ∧ ∨ ∨ ∧

2.
     ∧ ∨ ∧ ∨

3.
     ∧ ∧ — ∨

4.
     ∨ ∧ ∧ ∨

5.
     ∨ ∧ — ∧

6.
     ∧ ∨ ∨ ∧

7.
     ∧ ∨ — —

8.
     ∨ ∧ ∨ ∨

9.
     ∧ ∨ — ∨

10.
     ∧ ∧ ∨ ∨

CHAPTER 7

MATCHING:

1. B   2. F   3. E
4. D   5. A   6. C

DICTATION:

1.
∧ – ∧ ∨ ∨
r r m r d

2.
– ∨ ∨ ∧ ∨
m r d r d

3.
∧ ∨ ∨ ∧ ∨
m r d r d

4.
∧ ∧ ∨ ∨ –
r m r d d

5.
– ∧ – ∨ ∨
r m m r d

6.
∨ – ∧ ∨ ∨
r r m r d

CHAPTER 8

MATCAHING:

1. C   2. A   3. B   4. D

DICTATION:

1.
∧ – ∧ – ∨ᵥ
r r m m d

2.
∨ᵥ ∧ˆ ∨ᵥ ∧ ∨
d m d r d

3.
∧ ∨ ∨ ∧ˆ ∨ᵥ
m r d m d

4.
– ∧ ∨ᵥ ∧ ∨
r m d r d

5.
∧ˆ – ∨ ∨ –
m m r d d

6.
∨ᵥ ∧ ∧ ∨ᵥ –
d r m d d

REVIEW TEST

QUESTIONS:

1. pitch   2. ascending   3. descending   4. –
5. step   6. tonic sol-fa   7. skip

MATCHING:

8. B   9. A   10. D   11. C

IDENTIFYING:

12. ∧ˆ∨∧∨   13. ∨∨–∧ˆ   14. ––∧ˆ∨   15. ∨∧–∨ᵥ
16. ∧∧∨ᵥ∧   17. ∨–∨∧ˆ   18. ∨∨∧–   19. ∧ˆ∨–∧

DICTATION:

26.
d r m d r d
∧ ∧ ∨ᵥ ∧ ∨

27.
m d m m r d
∨ᵥ ∧ˆ – ∨ ∨

28.
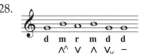
d m r m d d
∧ˆ ∨ᵥ ∧ ∨ᵥ –

29.
m d d r m r
∨ᵥ – ∧ ∧ ∨

30.
r r d m d m
– ∨ ∧ˆ ∨ᵥ ∧ˆ

31.

d d m r d m
– ∧ˆ ∨ ∧ ∧ˆ

32.
m r d r m m
∨ ∨ ∧ ∧ –

33.
d m m r r d
∧ˆ – ∨ – ∨

34.

r r m r m d
– ∧ ∨ ∧ ∨ᵥ

35.
d m m r d r
∧ˆ – ∨ ∨ ∧

36.
d r m r d m
∧ ∧ ∨ ∧ˆ

37.
d m r d d d
∧ˆ ∨ ∨ – –